Excess Baggage

Poetry Inspired by Life's Adventures

Kerri Read

To Leemon,

*I travelled the whole world searching for love,
only to find it back where I started.*

*After a lifetime of fitting in everywhere but
belonging nowhere, this is the story of how
I found my way home.*

Contents

Porcelain Dolls

You can't control me anymore
as I've moved on,
left your face behind.
I'd never leave anyone who never hurt me
but can't stand and watch
as you cut trees down.
Winter winds may blow
and icy shields grow
but you'll never know
how it feels to be torn.
Why can't you be happy
with flowers and sunshine?
All the time
you demanded a world
with so much more
when what you had
was wanted by all.
And even if I were to sing
and she to shine,
all you wanted from us
was to cover your lies.

To be pawns in your game.
To control the same way
as murderers do murder
and rapists do rape.
As if blood were just tears
and tears mere blood,
you frightened and sickened,
held hostage your blood.
Never once considered
the rapid results
as you panicked and pained
your porcelain dolls.

Alleys of Rust

Look at me, still running,
not sure what from.
Don't know where to,
through these alleys of rust.

Watch me, still praying;
anticipating,
hoping you're listening
as my head hits the dust.

Still checking shadows
and flirting with danger.
Still undressing my wounds
and swallowing up
so many ideas,
so much that's not clear;
as I sit and wonder
why love is just lust?

When will it find me?
When will you save me?
Stop playing games,
let the noise turn to haze.

Whisper your secret,
and how I can keep it.
Have me believe it
through your quiet gaze.

Mirage

I'm not missing you.
I'm missing the expected,
I'm missing what I wanted
and what you never gave.
Sold out and empty,
all that I'm missing
is what I hoped I would feel
and that is the shame;
that I'm not missing you.
I'm missing the dream.
The illusion you shattered,
how I thought it should be.
No, I'm not missing you,
just the possibility
of lying in the sun
and dancing in the rain.
How could I miss you
when you have forgotten?
All I am missing
is the mirage that you made.

One-Way Ticket

They said I was brave to book a one-way ticket.

As if there was some kind of security
in the knowledge of coming home.

But where I came from wasn't as important to me
as where I could end up.

Colours

I took it all; my heart and my hope.
I boarded the plane
waving to home
and I whispered to myself
as the plane dropped down
(less an affirmation,
more a subtle grounding).
Until I forgot the naysayers,
spoke to soothsayers,
ate thalis by temples,
became sentimental,
rickshawed on roads that flowed like the Ganges,
went to the ashram and thought I'd never leave.
But it was tea in emerald fields,
ayurveda that healed,
hearing sitar dance with drums,
overwhelmed by the fun
and the colours that went on and on and on.

And I realised that they didn't whisper, they screamed.
They said remember us,
all you need are your clothes
and the things
that your heart already knows.
Don't forget to pause and absorb
because life is too short
and leave here all the things
that you think that you thought.

And with that, I never whispered again.

Wish You Were Here

It's a beautiful night
and I wish you were here
with me in the darkness
collecting my tears.

As they shimmer in starlight,
I pine for the moon.
My flaws seem so bright,
so clear in this room.

But I wish you were here
to stop me from sighing,
by holding me softly
and shushing my crying.

To un-break my heart
which is crumbling in pain.
To undo the hurt
that is haunting again.

You can't understand
and I am ashamed,
but I wish you were here
all the same.

Monsoon

Let the rain pour
and wash me clean
as I wait for the silence to come.
Wading through streams
of terracottas and greens
I throw away my umbrella,
and submit to the weather.
I don't want to stay dry
and it's useless to try,
the intent of wild sky
is so heavy today.
All-consuming,
but I must keep moving.
If I could reach it with a pin
this whole facade would cave in.
I cling to a signpost as rivers rush past
but at long last, I know I can swim.

City Life

They give me streetlights
that don't come close to gentle moonlight
and expect me to be impressed.
Waiting in anticipation
of an ardent awe that will never come.
How can it?
When the moonlight remains stable,
and doesn't try to sway me.
Just tells me it's OK and
calms me when I'm not.
They think that streetlights can bribe me
when I've basked under black skies
so, I ask them,
do I look like a moth?

Lost

Searching.
Frantic
and you can't find it;
that place that you were looking for
and before you know it
every travel book you own is on the floor.
Scattered.
Like pieces of a puzzle
that are in the wrong box
but they must have been appealing once
because you bought them and held onto
every place,
every plan.
But now you are lost.
Exhausted.

How can it be when there are so many maps,
you just can't find your way home?

Pot Holes

It's only a short flight away
but I chose to take the bus
because the wheels squeaked
and the window didn't open.
Because the smell of heat stung my face
and I could only communicate
to the person next to me
with smiles and nods.
How wonderful that a smile is the same in all languages.
The view was beautiful
and the road was full of potholes
overflowing with adventure.
Strangers,
all heading to the same place.
Half a day cramped into one tiny space
praying your bladder won't give up,
really makes you appreciate
the important things in life.

Emeralds

Drifting on an endless sea.
Turquoise green.
The picture of a dream I once had.
A dragon bursts out of Lagoon Blue
and weaves its way through
1000 islands.
So many emerald islands
and none of them belong to me.
The air is filled with magic
and breathing it in is a wish
made by my aching heart.
The whole world is a gift
but this,
this is no less than treasure
and I am torn apart,
weak from wondering why I'm allowed to see it.
The sights whisper.
I dive in.
The water sets me free.
Nothing,
not even this
compares to
the magnitude of gratitude.

All the World

Listen.
Just listen, you can hear it if you try;
beyond the hows, whats, wheres, and whys.
Beyond the raging things I read;
the tragedy on my news feed.
The weeping hearts and broken bones,
the fighting, gunfire, bombs, and drones.
The hate, the hurt that screams for healing.
The bitter, ignorant, and reeling.
All the world is on fire.
Now listen.
To what can't be said;
touch the floor with your forehead.
They say
the world cannot be fixed by praying
but they are wrong.
When you want to be heard
the thing to do first
is listen
and if you must speak;
speak quietly
and if you must show;
show gently.

This world is loud enough,
so listen.
Pause.
Put your head on that floor
and weep out all of the things
that you are angry for.
The ground is where you sob the loudest
even if you didn't know you would.
That is the place to let the noise go
and only then will you know
that it's quieter than you think.

Souvenirs

Where am I going now?
What is left that you think I haven't seen?
Through jagged edges, thorny hedges,
you took me there, I couldn't breathe.
And all of it a distant blur, a mirage perhaps,
a gentle err
whenever I have time to think;
to fall,
to dive,
to hide,
to sink.
But I took with me some souvenirs;
the awe I felt, the splash of tears.
The love, the shame, the calm, the fear,
the how-to leave when pain appears.
The how to run in utter sadness,
the leaving behind in urgent madness,
The goodbyes that were too often ruthless,
the *I'll be back's* that were always useless.
The running stopped; the hiding started.
A forceless habit; a heart departed.

Maybe I thought I didn't deserve you,
like love or stability,
a safe place to come home to.
But you followed me wherever I went,
you found me stubborn
with passive intent.
So much gratitude I had for just being alive,
but the sadness forced questions about fairness,
about why I was allowed to be utterly free.
Why did you let them go and instead keep me?
And I couldn't comprehend,
I could only try,
and it's not until now
that I understand why.

Fearless

I don't travel fearlessly
with beaming face
and plans of fun.
I don't fall into friendly groups
or laze around under the sun.
I often feel
the fizz of worry,
the everything that could go wrong.
It often leads to haste and hurry,
get out before
the darkness comes.
But the pull is stronger than the panic.
The world more wonderful than strange.
I sacrifice security for wonder.
The same is always worse than change.

Travelling is not just for the fearless but,

it *is* only for the brave.

Heavy

How can I come with you when
you don't even seem to notice
how heavy your bags are?
It's hard to move gently
when you choose to take everything with you.

What is the point of spontaneity
when your hands are so full
that they cannot catch
the beauty of it anymore?

Don't bring with you so many bags
hoping for others to carry them too.
Some of us prefer to travel light
and dwell in sheer simplicity.

Traveller's Prayer

Release my grip from what
you don't want me to take.
Let me walk away without a trace
of sorrow or regret,
Not spend a second more in vain,
holding on to what was never mine to keep.

Let me keep what you have had me gain.
Let me not react and push away,
play silly games;
capsizing at my own expense,
forgetting the rules altogether,
shivering because
I can't accept the warmth you offer.

Keep me safe from ships
that are going under in the dark of the night.
The things that lurk beneath the surface
waiting to eat me up,
and when face to face with what I fear
take my hand and lead me away.
I don't want to stay.

Keep me calm and sane
when you change the weather
and when the rain drinks me up
and has me heaving against wanton tides,
when I'm thrown against colourful arrays
of rusty rocks that show no mercy on pale skin;
let me swim.

Let me swim with strength,
with my head above the foam
then when the water calms
let me dive into depths
that I did not know were there.
There let me see the secrets of my heart.
The ones that hold the key
to a better me.

Kindness of Strangers

I couldn't stand on my own two feet
when you put me in your car.
You took me to a hotel
far from anywhere.
Dark and empty.
I lay in the space
where nightmares lived.
I didn't dare to waste a care
on where I was.
I wondered only,
if I would ever see the light.
But you left me water and sent up rice
and I got better.
I paid my bill
but to this day still,
I wish I knew who you were.

Almost

Just for a moment,
I thought I knew your name.
Could've sworn by the fact
that I recognised your face.
Lively eyes at peace,
gentle soul
standing its ground.
A familiar feeling.
Remembering the sound
of footsteps on the shore
and crushed ice against a glass.
The slamming of a door.
Taking off the mask.
But I lost it all again,
or was it stolen away?
I almost had it back,
I was almost me again.

Sunset

I thought that my heart didn't know love
although my eyes could see it,
and my soul could sense it,
and my ears could hear it
everywhere.
Everywhere
beautiful wonders
in patterns and codes
that only an open mind could know.
And I knew that love existed
because of the way the trees protect
the flowers from the rain
and because of the sunset,
the magnificent fading
only to return again
in case somebody missed it.
And I saw that little girl give the old lady her seat,
and I saw the little dog hold a baby bird
between its feet
so that the cats couldn't get it.

But I didn't want to be that girl
who sat alone on the beach.
Saddened by waves
that grew quiet as the sky blurred
with its reds and golden browns.
So I stayed back under palm trees instead as she cried,
and through her echoing sobs,
I tried to figure out why some people
just couldn't feel it, without even realising
that I was one who could.

Unrequited

You and your wings,
those wings of gold.
They carry you so high
from the ground below.
From here you look
like a butterfly.
How can you not know?

Didn't you stop to ask
where you were going to?
Didn't you stop to look around
and see who was watching you?
Didn't you wonder why
your heart was on the ground
while you were soaring high?

But you never even noticed;
you just carried on,
soaking up the storm.
You just kept on rising,
freezing out the warm.

And you never even noticed
me and my net following below,
in case you were to fall.
Holding up my dreams
as if they were a flower.

Waiting for you to land.

Coming Home

It had been such a long time.
So many calls, over so many miles
and I thought that we would sit
and drink coffee in the sun,
catching up on months of fun.
Maybe it was the time that altered my perception.
Or hearing about other people's receptions.
You see, I didn't expect a red carpet or fanfare,
I just thought that maybe you would be pleased
I was there.
But in the end,
through gritted teeth,
I just counted down the hours.
Me sitting in the sun,
you planting all your flowers.
The milk was sour.
There was no warmth
in my coffee cup.
Everything I offered was spat out,
chewed up.
I tried. I really did.
Maybe I'd been away too long.

Now, everything I said was wrong.
I know you have your reasons.
That life left you behind.
That you were stuck in changing seasons
and the weather was unkind.
But that was not my fault.
I just misjudged the tone,
and thought that maybe you could be happy
I was coming home.

Green Birds

My mouth is made from mud
and my heart is made of stone.

My legs are made of air
and my arms are just on loan.

My head, it doesn't care
and my eyes, they never weep.

My ears refuse to hear
and my mind just does not sleep.

If you should try to touch me, you might just understand
that hopes and dreams are scattered in another land,
where waterfalls splash freely
over grass that's lustrous green
and little birds, they know of things
that you have never seen.

And when I hear them sing
that song my heart; it turns to sand.
From fear of what I'll never do or in hope of what I can.

Sometimes I don't know the difference.

Sometimes panic pushes in.

Sometimes my footing fails me.

But like those birds,
I choose to sing.

Little Towns

Take me back to little towns of blue and white.
Where travelling feet meet cobbled streets with ease,
and with wind in hair, without a care, I am free.

There is not a sight that compares
to the sparkling ripples on the sea.
Bright bougainvillea dancing in breeze.
Pink and pretty, please, take me back.

Leave me there if you must but let me breathe.
Deep breaths in of salty air while
I share plates of food that make me feel like I am home.

Oh, how I long to roam those pretty streets above the sea.
Don't wait for me, I'm already there.

People Watching

She sits and watches worlds go by.
A solemn glance that never stares
but measures every minute detail
of pasts and presents
while they are unaware
of her crucial interest.
They all go about their way,
indifferent.
Just one common thing remains.
They are all alike,
eyes glued to the floor
wrapped up in their lives
considering nothing more.
But she in her corner,
looks out on a place
where the simplest
yet most beautiful things
are wasted.
To some, it would simply
never occur
to acknowledge the few who see people.

Like her.

Itchy Feet

What are words?
These wings that flutter,
faintly stutter,
stirring up
all connotations,
worlds of madness,
single sadness
at dewy dusk.
Where are you going?
In darkened dampness
with worry hampered,
shrivelling up
and beating thunder
beckons yonder
but the sea it calls,
so go you must.

Belonging

I don't belong in bustling cities.
Winding streets
and sights that sing.
Malls that shine
and mountain-tops.
With relics or with shiny things.

I don't belong in seaside towns,
in fishing boats,
or slick hotels.
I don't belong in skyscrapers.
In desert sands.
Among bluebells.

But anywhere can feel like home
if you stay long enough.

Acceptance

Heaviness washes over
in waves and lucid rhymes
that murmur between spaces
leaving limbs helpless every time.

Some things we cannot conquer
and of those this is just one.
Some things we try to fight for
and from others, try to run.

But running makes the pain worse
and here is pain enough.
Hearts should not be waged as weapons
when the yellow road turns tough.

Notice how the coast knows
that its neighbour is washing it away
and that it's getting weaker
every single day.

Yet it still stands strong.
In gentle acceptance,
and each time it crumbles
it does so in repentance.

Ask the tree who knows that
the air that lets it live
could uproot its very being
but still, it only gives.

It never asks for anything,
simply takes what it is given.
Even birds know that they will sing
long after they stop living.

New Year's Eve

Explosions of pink and champagne fizz
over Sydney harbour bridge.
Alive with wishes for a better year
as people cheer.

But I can only taste the smoke,
the sizzling glow of wasted hope,
and crowds of things I never spoke
from crippling fear.

Bursts of chances left to take.
Spirals of the things at stake.
Choices that weren't mine to make
in the first place.

Now that the countdown is done
there's nowhere left for me to run.
How is it possible here for anyone
to be this alone?

Moving On

Listening to sad songs across a faulty wire.
The words crackle and the tune breaks.
My words can't find an escape.
I'm so sick of sitting in run-down internet cafes,
just drinking coffee by myself.

I want to know why
I'm waiting here.
How so much has happened?
How time can move so fast
in places where everything stays the same.
So here I am packing bags again,
chasing sunshine for the last time.

Tulips

Take me to that place
where I want to stay forever,
where it's safe and I can melt
but melting is never enough.
And my beating heart, won't be happy
until it's wrapped around another.
Let me lose myself and forget about the weather.
Whether it's pouring, flooding drops of rain
or searing sun won't matter then.
Because rain can only cleanse
and sun can only soothe,
and when it rains it pours
but at least then the birds eat well.
And when the sun shines,
the flowers grow
and I am growing with them.

I didn't mean to make you see me
where I am not.
Nor did I have a say in searching the globe
and finding you back where I started.
If I had a say, I would have saved my time
and never left at all.

Time is precious you see,
and so much time is spent
in this field of petals.
And it's the whispers of the breeze
that keeps me going back.
I have let myself hope
that you are there too;
welcoming the wilting,
while we wait with the naivety of children
touching tulips for the first time.

The View

I never thought the view could be better than this,
jagged rock falling into deep blue bliss.
Green tumbling from the sky's warm kiss
and the birds soaring free.
Just how they should be.

Nobody for miles, I smile at the scene.
At how lucky I am, how lucky I've been.
Hashtag "blessed," I write on my screen,
what more in the world could I need?

But older and wiser, I need to go back again.
To see that view from my memory reframed.
All of the edges, the greens and the blues
because better than seeing it alone,
would be seeing it with you.

Desert

They call it empty.
Once a dried-up bed of sea
but it's only in the vastness
that I ever truly feel like me.

Breathing in the heavy air
that smothers lungs with heat.
Escarpments run for miles.
The isolation sets you free.

Stories from before time
carved out by rain and air.
Where tiny things survive in sand
and footprints disappear.

Is there anything more real
than the relentless heat?
Anything more full of the world
than the sand beneath our feet?

All else is but a whisper.
A passing drop in time.
A shimmering mirage
that's impossible to find.

Fall

Fallen leaves trampled with sudden sadness
disintegrate from fleeting madness.

The sky is clear and filled with warmth,
dry eyes are seeing what they have been taught.

My heart feels like it could almost believe it
and skin is cold but no one can feel it.

If only the plan was less sporadic.
If its pace slowed and lost its panic.

If the grasp could loosen and I could be trusted
to not get too overly excited.

But the fear runs as deep as quiet, still waters,
it took me down paths that I'd not even thought of,

and I have learned that I'm not so cold.
That there are intricate depths to this complex soul.

I am not so battered and broken and bruised
to be deaf to the beauty and blind to the truth.

As the music plays and the wall starts to shatter,
you watch me wait to see what matters.

You are smiling because you know better than me
the fate of those trampled fallen leaves.

The Sea

I asked you to take me to the sea.
You thought it strange but you agreed
and were happy just to be near me
although the coast wasn't where you would choose to be.

We arrived.
You tried to see the attraction.
But in failing, I made a welcome distraction as
I stared longingly at the crashing waves.
In awe. At peace.
You were unamazed.

But waves are strong and unafraid, they build
then crash, then fade away.
At once intense then calmly quiet,
a soothing sense after a passionate riot.
While the sand stands, sincere, unchanging.
Honest, loyal, uncomplaining.

The waves draw the sand to its deepest depths
and the sand doesn't so much as protest.
The waves throw their shit to the safety of the shore
and the sand just accepts while the waves demand more.

They push, they pull,
they come and they go,
but the sand just smiles
because it knows
that the crashing won't last
and the calmness will come,
so it stays in the rain
and it stays in the sun.

How would the sea fare with nowhere to rest?
And what would the shore be without waves on its chest?

As we waited in the cold
being sprayed by the air
you hummed a tune in your head as I sat there.

You had never really seen the sea before.
That was one of the things that you loved me for.
Then you asked me *why?*
When I said I loved you more;
it's because I am the sea
and you are the shore.

Boats

I'd go with you anywhere
because you make my heart smile
and my mind calm.
With you, it feels like the colour yellow
resting on a turquoise sea
without a care
that the house is falling in.

Why should I care when my glass is full
and the sky is soft and blue?
When I can see the boats that travel
far against the tide
but come home in the end
safe and content?

And it's almost like they never left,
except their nets are full,
so suddenly.

How it happened is forgotten,
unimportant are the hows against the lesson.

Uncomplicated.

As if the situation always knew that it would be.
As if I was always waiting for you
and you were waiting for me.

Waiting

I don't travel anymore.
I sit and wait behind closed doors,
like a passport without the ink,
I cannot plan, I cannot think.
Fixed to a bed
that's not felt the heaviness of sleep,
my heart won't take unless it can keep,
and I haven't heard
the stories of dreams.
In the distance, another adventure screams.
It warns of the pain of pining panic
and the mundane turns into quiet manic
as the wanting subsides
I know now's not the time
but the time is too slow
and the waiting it knows.
How can I go anywhere new
when I am stuck and cannot move?

Sleeping Lions

The sun had long seen its last shadow
and trees had finished their last prayers.
The flowers, safely in their caskets
waiting for the morning air.

She crept slowly through the quiet
silhouettes of familiar things.
Body heavy from the manic,
head racing with what tomorrow brings.

Softly she breezed into the calm
of that place where her heart could heave
and paused as she heard a purr,
of her lions in their deep sweet peace.

Each breath as beautiful as the other
her mind drifted to the first.
Thankful she got to fall asleep
to the best sound on earth.

Love

I didn't know until tonight
how much I love you.
Like a bird taking flight
the breeze caught my heart
and the pain came
so softly.
As we giggled in bed
about something, you'd said.
I crumbled in sweet surrender
and I wondered what we'd look like
10 years from now.
With laughter lines
and grey hairs,
shrugs,
smiles,
and a million cares.
At that moment I knew
that wherever you go,
I'll be coming too,
just praying that I will always love you
as much as I do today.

Five Suitcases

Today I packed my whole life into five suitcases.

Begrudgingly at first.

Half of those were toys
that the kids couldn't say goodbye to,
so I swapped out treasured books
and clothes sewn with sentiment
for pieces of plastic that were the bane of my life.

Because their world was already chaotic enough
and if shiny dolls and worn-out bears
could make it more familiar, then so be it.
Anything for them.
Even packing my life into five suitcases
to move halfway across the world.

Sand

They told me I would find
nothing but sand.
A sea of black.
Oppression.
Isolation
got the better of me;
I ventured out,
although I felt a
colourful oddity.
But all I found
was the depth of coffee,
the sweetness of dates,
and the warmth of the sun.
The simplicity of black and white
and how to feel comfortable in my skin.
How depressing it must be to see only sand
in a place this full of life.

Airports

I'm coming home.
Had packed before the phone took its last ring.
Just myself, my passport,
there wasn't time to think of things.
I'm holding back a waterfall of sadness in my heart.
Grief and hope fight it out,
tearing numbness apart.
I usually love airports,
full of movement and life,
I never really thought about the people inside.
I hear a happy phone call,
a father going home.
A mother enjoying the quiet of all alone.
The happy, heaving cases
of a family on vacation,
their excitement is so loud
and even I can't blame them.
But memories of you come
and squeeze out of my eyes,
I turn to watch the planes
in a hopeless effort to hide.

Just praying that I'll get there in time.

Just Visiting

I said I was coming home
and when I got there,
I found not the warm hug of tea
but the crumbs at the bottom of the cup.
I thought it would be
different somehow.
That I'd feel more like me,
and all the things I had been missing
would patch me up.
But in between the gaps of conversations,
the ageing faces,
and the taller kids,
I decided that now
I prefer coffee instead.

The Moon

I planned a trip to the moon.
You rolled your eyes
and looked away.
You didn't want the stars.
Just to play with a little white cat in the sand.
Watching it leap and land.
Chasing ribbons through the breeze,
down a slide,
up a tree.
You only wanted the coolness of the ground.
The grass on bare legs,
the joy of bird sounds.
And I was too blinded by the sun to see that
that was all you needed.

Grown Ups

Why is it only when grey hairs grow
you find out
that nobody really knows
what they are doing?
Year after year,
over dinner, you hear
that everyone has it hard,
carrying scraps of useless paper and
regret amongst their credit cards.
The things they've given away.
The things that they have taken.
Made too many mistakes and
left either stirred or shaken.
Everyone is scared of something
or maybe even everything.
Some people silence the noise
while others listen to birds sing.
Why does it take so long
for us to realise
that we are only human after all?

Home

It's a strange thing:
24 hours.
Yesterday I sat at your place
full heart, warm sun on my face
drinking coffee and laughing as if we were home.

I cried when we left
but it didn't really sink in until today.
A whole continent between us.
And now I'm putting suitcases away until next year.
The only difference was a plane.
A plane and a day.
But isn't it strange?

Out of sight out of mind.
A whole life left behind.
Not sure which is real, not sure which is mine.
Hearts are not cut out to choose.
What a sacrifice, they say.
But living this way means there is always something
to look forward to.

The Circle of Life

I love it when the weekend comes
and I can stay with you.
I spend the week thinking about
all the fun things we will do.
Making cakes with lots of jam
and eating them with tea,
saving all the best bits
and giving them to me.
Bubbling soups that smell like home
and fudge that's super sweet.
Making headbands out of daisies
and dresses out of sheets.
Net curtain trains for wedding dresses.
Daffodils in a posey.
Sitting in bed chatting
so that we are nice and cosy.
Teaching me the names of all
the birds, trees, and flowers.
Walking along those country lanes
for what felt like hours and hours.
Feeding horses with the carrots
you couldn't use for dinner.

Playing 'in my bag I packed'
and letting me be the winner.
Telling me all about
the wonderful places you have been,
mountains, lakes, and sunsets,
all the things I've never seen.

But one day I will get a little older suddenly,
and there might be some other places that I'd rather be;
out with friends, starting work,
or studying for tests.
And that's the way life's meant to be
when life is done best.

But one day I'll turn up again
and make you tea with cake too,
and I'll save the best bits
and give them all to you.
Maybe I will cook something
like bubbling soup for lunch
and when I see some daffodils
I will buy you a whole bunch.

I'll show you pictures of
my wedding dress and gold jewellery set
and you will think of me dressed up
in daisies and window nets.
You will ask me to check the internet
for the names of some new flowers
and I will talk much like before,
for hours and hours.
Sometimes, I will bring you something new
I cooked for dinner
and you will play 'I Spy'
and let my children be the winners.
Then we'll tell you all about
the wonderful places that we've been;
skyscrapers, pyramids, dolphins,
all the things you've never seen.

Then one day you'll get a little older suddenly
and there might be some other place
that you have to be
and when that happens, I will think of you
riding a horse along a beach

or sitting in a garden filled
with bursts of pink and peach.
Wherever you go I know
that you'll be sitting drinking tea too,
as I drink mine and think
of all the things we used to do.

Distance

I hope when we are old,
when our time comes,
that this is how we leave;
together, like this.
In some place we call home with the
heaviness of gratitude on our hearts.
Written in wrinkles;
stories of all the places we have been.
Hearts mapped with memories
of the whole world
but even this close
feels like too much distance.
I hold your hand to my face and
think to myself,
what a poem this would make
but as it twitches
I realise that I am gripping too hard,
I let go
and decide that words can wait.

Little Bird

Was it so long ago
that drops of crystal air fell on open lungs
and eyes sparkled as they drank in the sea?
Was it that long ago
that my heart tingled and my smile beamed?
That I was so totally free?
Where did she go?
That little bird who flew away in search of truth?
Maybe she found it.
Or died trying.
Either way,
I wish she'd come back.

Road Trip

I don't know who I am half the time,
mum, mess of a person, wife.
Just stumbling through life.
Falling over toys that I didn't want to buy in the first place.

But then we get in the car.
Familiarity is far and
I can't see the chaos behind me.
Spilt bags of candy,
legs that are sandy
and everything we need for a week.

I see only the open road.
The joy that I've known
and we talk, singing songs
like we only just met and
yet our hearts set,
together forever.

Who knows where we'll end up
when every turn is a surprise?
Every change of scenery,
more beautiful than the last time.
Are we nearly there yet? Little voices cry,
and so suddenly I realise
that 'not quite' there yet
is my favourite place to be.

Fort

I run around complaining about the mess.
You'll miss it when they are older
I try to convince myself.
But today I only see the stress.
A million barriers to
the places I'd have been,
the things I could have seen.

You built a fort.
Come in and play.
Suddenly I'm hit by a
a bittersweet pang of regret,
guilt perhaps,
then despair
that the time moves too fast.
Forget opportunities long past,
one day
I won't be able to make myself small enough
to crawl on my knees
to this cosy space
where dreams live.

Then it hits me like a cannonball.
Bam.
From nowhere.
One day
there won't be a fort at all.
The chairs will stay
sternly in their places
and quilts in cupboards.
Folded neat and clean.
Fun hidden away.
Life tidy,
and stress-free.

So today I decided to play.

Some People

I never understood why some people love parks.
Predictable and tended to,
pathways clearly marked so that you can't detour
into the vulnerable.
Where's the fun in that?

Once, I wanted the vastness of the desert,
the silence of sand scattering in the wind.
Relentless reality.
If you can't see beauty in the harshness
then at least you begin to understand life.

I always loved the ocean,
to dive into the deep and be swept away.
The magnetism of velvet nothingness.
But the depths are where the treasures are, and
tides always change.

I thought I would never meet the meadow.
Wildflowers, refreshing and real.
The mellow ease of green and yellow
But then I walked in fields
that felt like the breeze.

And now I know, it's not about the places
that you go but the people you are with.

Ceasefire

What have we done?
In this place here,
where the eyes do not cry
and the heart has no fear.

Where there used to be kindness,
beauty, and meaning.
Where there used to be helping,
healing, and breathing.

Now lives are just numbers
and bodies in the way,
and nobody ever seems to pay.

Where difference is an excuse
to justify hate.
To take and take
and never replace.

We wish and we will,
and pray for some still
but they bomb.

Kill.
Break.
Spill.

"Enough is Enough".

Feeling helpless?
Tough.

Even hope feels like dust in the wind.

City of Roses

High up on a mountain-top,
far away from *whys* and *whats,*
she scans a sky in azure blue
as she thinks in twists and knots.

She meant to simply walk today
but things turned out a different way.
Now here she was, almost lost,
watching day and night in play.

Took the freshness in each stride
and watched a tiny stream splash by,
hardly thriving, just surviving,
now she began to cry.

She willed it around massive rocks,
foliage and thick grass blocks.
Making its way on in hope,
oblivious to the clock.

She panicked once she came to know
the deep dark hole that stopped its flow
until she saw that where it stopped
was the place where flowers grow.

The Art of Doing Nothing

Today I will not shower,
there's no time for necessity.
Instead, I'll dig a hole
where it looks like a plant should be.
I'll give in to the craving
to blurt out an inner poem.
To research the history
of places far from home.
Today I'll drink some coffee
and close my eyes under the sun.
I'll blast my music loud
and dance around in whirls of fun.
I'll sing the same song 16 times
and still forget the words.
I'll use the internet to find out
things I've never heard.
The doorbell will ring,
and a delivery will distract me.
I'll open it and then forget
where I put it exactly.
I'll search for a pen only to forget
what I wanted it for
but by then I'll be knee-deep
in tidying messy drawers.

Dinner time approaches
and some urgency kicks in.
I'll fly around the kitchen
grabbing pots and pans and tins.
I'll empty the fridge
of almost everything in there
and I'll create the most beautiful
recipe to share.
As it cooks, I'll quickly *just* fix
that leaky tap.
I'll search how long it takes
to walk to Riyadh and back.
Then I remember that I'm supposed
to go out tonight.
I guess a shower wouldn't hurt
and by now I'm quite the sight.
My friend will call and say
that soon she will be coming
and when she asks what I've been doing today
I'll say
"Absolutely nothing."

Excess Baggage

I am eternally stamped
by the places I've been,
the stories of the people
I've met along the way.

A suitcase packed full
of the sights that I've seen.
The loss that made me leave
and the love that made me stay.

Stories stuffed in bags
that are bursting at the seams.
Dragging around details
that no longer serve my days.

The experiences that made me
who I'm meant to be.
Awestruck and wild
and wonderfully free.

But time flies by
as if my life was on screen
and the longer I'm gone
the heavier it weighs.

It's about time I let
this excess baggage be,
and work on travelling light
as I find my way.

Acknowledgements

To my mum,

I'm sorry for all the stress I must have caused you with my need to travel and spontaneous trips. Thank you for always being there when I came home.

To my husband,

Thank you for accepting me just the way I am and encouraging me to follow my dreams no matter how crazy they may be. Everything is more wonderful when I'm with you.

To my children,

Seeing the world through your eyes has been the most beautiful adventure of all. I can't wait to see where the world takes you.

To my late nanny,

You sparked my love of nature, scenery and sunsets. Thank you for always listening to my poetry.

To my friends,

I would not be me without the coffees, long walks, and deep conversations.

I am so grateful for you all.

About the Author

Kerri has always been passionate about travel. Even as a child, despite knowing nothing of the world she always knew that she needed to see it. She took her first solo trip at 16 and hasn't stopped travelling since. She has visited over 30 countries and has lived and worked in 4 continents. She currently lives in Saudi Arabia with her husband, three children and a few rescue cats. As well as travelling at any opportunity, she spends her time writing, drinking iced coffee, and encouraging others to get out and see more of the world around them.